A HISTORICAL ALBUM OF
ALABAMA

A HISTORICAL ALBUM OF

ALABAMA

Charles A. Wills

THE MILLBROOK PRESS, Brookfield, Connecticut

Front and back cover: Untitled rural scene. Painting by Xanthus Smith. Private Collection.

Title page: Sunset on the eastern shore of Mobile Bay, Fairhope Municipal Pier.
   Photograph by Dan Brothers. Courtesy of the Alabama Bureau of Tourism & Travel.

Library of Congress Cataloging-in-Publication Data

Wills, Charles.
   A historical album of Alabama / Charles A. Wills.
      p.   cm. — (Historical albums)
   Includes index.
   Summary: A history of Alabama, from its early exploration and
settlement to the state today.
      ISBN 1-56294-591-2 (lib. bdg.) ISBN 1-56294-854-7 (pbk.)
      1. Alabama—History—Juvenile literature. 2. Alabama—
Gazetteers—Juvenile literature. I. Title.   II. Series.
F326.3.W55 1995
976.1—dc20   95-11774
                                                  CIP
                                                  AC

Created in association with Media Projects Incorporated

   C. Carter Smith, *Executive Editor*
   Kimberly Horstman, *Project Editor*
   Charles A. Wills, *Principal Writer*
   Bernard Schleifer, *Art Director*
   John W. Kern, *Production Editor*
   Arlene Goldberg, *Cartographer*

   Consultant: Dr. Robert J. Norrell, Professor of History,
   The University of Alabama, Tuscaloosa, Alabama

Manufactured in the United States of America

10 9 8 7 6 5 4 3 2 1

CONTENTS

Introduction

Alabama is a state of surprises.

It is a Southern state—but unlike other Southern states, its earliest settlers were not from England but from France and Spain. Many people think of New Orleans, Louisiana, another American city with French roots, as home of the Mardi Gras celebration, but the festival has been celebrated in Mobile since the 1700s.

For much of its history, Alabama was a mostly rural state with an economy based on cotton—and yet in the 1880s and 1890s, before heavy industry came to the rest of the South, Alabama had its own "industrial revolution," centered in the iron furnaces of Birmingham.

Even today many people think of Alabama as a quiet state of pine forests, farms, and small towns—and yet it was the engineers and scientists at Redstone Arsenal in Huntsville that launched America into the space age in the 1950s.

Alabama's story, however, is also a story of struggle—especially the struggle of the state's African Americans to free themselves from a system of segregation (separation by race), and to enjoy the rights they were entitled to as American citizens. No state played a more important part in the civil rights movement of the 1950s and 1960s than Alabama, from the Montgomery Bus Boycott in 1956 to Martin Luther King, Jr.'s, march on Selma in 1964.

Together, all these elements make Alabama's history a rich and dramatic story.

THE HEART OF DIXIE

Swiss artist Carl Bodmer painted this view of a Choctaw camp. Choctaw dwellings were usually built with a frame of wood poles topped with a roof of thatched grass or reeds; the sides were sometimes plastered with a mixture of clay and crushed shells.

Alabama was inhabited by a great Native American civilization, the Mississippians, when the first Spanish explorers reached the region in the 1500s. Later, numerous Native American groups—the Cherokees, Chickasaws, Choctaws, and Creeks—emerged from the declining Mississippian culture. France planted the first colony on Alabama soil—a fur-trading post near present-day Mobile. In the 1700s, control of the area passed to Britain and then to the young United States. After the power of Alabama's Native Americans was destroyed in the Creek War (1814), the region became a territory (1817) and a state (1819), and wealth from cotton brought prosperity. Alabama was part of the Confederacy during the Civil War and suffered greatly both in that war and in its bitter aftermath.

The First Alabamians

In 1957, archaeologists working in Russell Cave in northern Alabama made an important discovery. Digging patiently through layers of soil and debris, they found ancient tools—a spear point made of bone, a lamp made from the leg bone of a bear—dating back thousands of years. Not far from the tools, they found the bones of a man—one of the oldest sets of human remains found in North America.

The ancestors of this prehistoric Alabamian had come originally from Asia. They had crossed to North America on a land bridge, now vanished, that connected the two continents. Over thousands of years, these newcomers, whose descendants became the Native Americans, spread out across North America. By about 7000 B.C., they had reached what is now Alabama.

These ancient peoples are called Paleo Indians. ("Paleo" means old, and "Indian" was the name mistakenly given to Native Americans by early European explorers.) The Paleo Indians survived by hunting the animals, many now extinct, that roamed the region's forests. They lived in natural shelters like Russell Cave.

Over time, the Paleo Indian Culture became more advanced and was known as the Archaic Culture.

Alabama's Archaic Indians hunted for food, but they also gathered wild plants to eat. Eventually they began growing corn and vegetables on land cleared of trees.

The Paleo Indians and Archaic Peoples were mostly nomadic—they moved from place to place in search of food. By around 1000 B.C., however, Alabama's early peoples had mastered farming and developed better tools and weapons. They began to settle in permanent villages. This was the beginning of the society that scholars call the Woodland Culture.

As time passed, the Woodland Peoples of Alabama and the rest of the Mississippi River Valley grew more sophisticated. Tribes—groups of people, usually related, who lived together in villages—began to trade with one another. Small villages grew into substantial towns that often centered around high mounds of earth.

These mounds, some as high as sixty feet, were the focus of the Woodland Peoples' religious life. Many were topped with temples or the homes of important leaders. Others served as burial sites for the dead. Nearly forty of these structures can still be found in Alabama at Mound State Monument near the town of Moundville.

This mound-building society, often called the Mississippian Culture, stretched from what is now Illinois to the Gulf of Mexico and lasted from about A.D. 800 to 1500. By the time

The Native Americans of the Southeast created many beautiful objects for use in everyday life or religious rituals. The intricate design of this stone palette (right), probably used for painting, features two rattlesnakes.

As many as 3,000 people may have lived around the Great Mound at Moundville (below) during Mississippian times. Some historians believe the mounds were inspired by contact with the great civilizations of Mexico and Central America, such as the Aztecs and Olmecs.

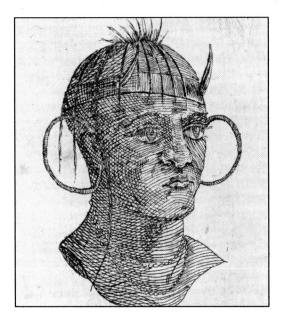

This engraving of a Creek war chief appeared in a book published in 1775. At the time, the Creeks were the most powerful Native American nation in the Southeast, with as many as 3,500 warriors scattered throughout Creek villages in Georgia, Alabama, and Florida.

the first European explorers arrived in Alabama, however, the Mississippian Culture was beginning to disappear.

The reasons for this decline are still unknown, but historians believe the Mississippian population may have grown too fast for their food supply. What remained of the Mississippian Peoples was destroyed in wars with early European explorers, and by the diseases, especially smallpox, that the explorers brought with them.

In the 1600s and 1700s, new Native American peoples, thought to be descendants of the temple mound builders, emerged in Alabama. These tribes spoke the Muskhogean language and, after joining with smaller tribes in the region, developed into the Creek Confederacy.

The name "Alabama" comes from the name of one of the groups in the Creek Confederacy—the Alibamu tribe. For many years, historians believed that Alibamu meant "here we rest" or "the good land where we rested." Modern scholars now think the tribe's name is better translated as "the brush clearers," from the practice of clearing land for the planting of corn, beans, squash, tobacco, and other crops.

Creek villages were organized into Red towns and White towns. The Red towns were home to warriors, who were in charge of carrying out attacks on other tribes. All war dances were held in the Red town. The tribe's peacemakers lived in the White town. Here, treaties with neighboring tribes were written and signed.

Other Muskhogean-speaking peoples included the Choctaws, who lived in southern Alabama and along the Tombigbee River, and the warlike Chickasaws, the Choctaws' northern neighbors.

The last major Native American group to settle in Alabama were the Cherokees. An Iroquois-speaking people, the Cherokees left their original homeland in what is now Georgia in the 1700s to escape the pressure of white settlement.

Like other Southeastern tribes, the Cherokees relied on farming and wild plants for much of their diet. In addition, they hunted wild game, such as deer and bears, with bows and arrows. In order to get close to a deer without scaring it away, hunters would drape themselves with entire deerskins, including the antlers, and use deer calls to lure the animals.

The Creeks, Choctaws, Chickasaws, and Cherokees were excellent farmers and craftsworkers who lived in well-organized villages. Early white settlers called these peoples the "five civilized tribes" (the fifth were the Seminoles in neighboring Florida) because of their accomplishments, and also because of their willingness to adopt the settlers' ways.

In this painting by George Catlin, Choctaw men play *chunkee*, a game similar to lacrosse. Sometimes Choctaw villages competed against each other in great tournaments. Although using the sticks to fight was not allowed, the game was physically brutal and many people suffered injuries and even death during the matches.

The French and Spanish Eras

We do not know the identity of the first Europeans to set foot in Alabama or to see its shores. Rough outlines of the Alabama coastline appeared on European maps as early as 1505, not long after Christopher Columbus's first voyage to the lands Europeans called the New World. The first European known to have visited Alabama was Alonso Álvarez de Piñeda, who explored Mobile Bay in 1519.

Twenty years later, a much larger Spanish *entrada* (expedition) landed at Tampa Bay in Florida. Its leader was Hernando de Soto, the governor of Cuba. With 700 men, de Soto marched north as far as present-day Tennessee, then south into Alabama.

In their search for gold, de Soto's soldiers ransacked Native American villages and cruelly mistreated the inhabitants. By the time they entered Alabama in October 1540, the region's Native Americans knew what to expect from the Spanish.

De Soto soon clashed with Tascalusa, a great chief of the Mississippian Peoples. At the village of Mabila, Tascalusa's warriors launched a surprise attack on the Spanish. Bloody fighting raged for hours; when it was over, many of de Soto's men and thousands of Indians lay dead.

The surviving Spanish escaped, made their way out of Alabama, and

Clad in armor and carrying pikes and matchlock muskets, men of Hernando de Soto's expedition wade through a swamp on their trip across the Southeast. This painting by Frederic Remington appeared in *Collier's Weekly* nearly 400 years after de Soto's journey.

reached safety in Mexico three years later. De Soto was not among them. He died on the banks of the Mississippi River in 1542.

The first attempt at founding a Spanish colony in Alabama came in 1559, when 1,000 settlers led by Tristan de Luna landed at Mobile Bay. Hunger and disease ravaged the colonists, however, and after three years the survivors gave up and returned to Mexico.

The misfortunes of de Soto's expedition and the failure of de Luna's colony led the Spanish to abandon their colonizing efforts along the Gulf of Mexico. For more than a century, the region's Indians were left alone.

But the Spanish left behind an unwelcome reminder of their presence: disease. Thousands of Native Americans died of smallpox and other diseases brought by the Spanish and by the European traders that occasionally visited the Gulf Coast.

A new chapter in Alabama's history opened in 1689, when Robert Cavalier, Sieur de La Salle, journeyed down the Mississippi River to the Gulf of Mexico. La Salle claimed all the land drained by the Mississippi, including Alabama, for France. He named the vast territory Louisiana to honor France's king, Louis XIV.

In 1698, two brothers, Pierre Le Moyne, Sieur d'Iberville, and Jean-Baptiste Le Moyne, Sieur de Bienville, took charge of Louisiana. The region's first settlement was in present-day Mississippi, but in 1702 the brothers moved Louisiana's "capital" to the banks of the Mobile River in Alabama. After a flood in 1711, the settlement moved again, this time to a site close to the mouth of Mobile Bay.

The colony's early years were difficult. Hunger and disease claimed the lives of many settlers. The colonists, mostly soldiers, also suffered raids by English pirates and an attack by Spanish settlers from Pensacola, Spain's colony on Florida's Gulf Coast.

Few Frenchmen and women were willing to settle in the remote and dangerous colony. To provide wives for the colonists, the French government sent a shipload of poor young women to Mobile in 1704. They were called *filles de cassette*, or cassette girls, because each was given a cassette (small trunk) of clothes before leaving France.

The Le Moyne brothers hoped to trade with local people for furs, but the Native Americans stayed away from the settlement. Over time, however, the French won the confidence of the Indians, and a flourishing fur trade began.

Some French colonists began to plant crops of sugar, rice, and indigo (a plant that produced a natural dye) for sale in Europe. To care for these crops, about 600 African slaves were brought to Mobile in 1619—the beginning of almost two and a half centuries of slavery in the region.

Because the planters grew cash

crops instead of food, hunger remained a threat in Mobile. In 1720, the colony came close to starvation, but gifts of food from the Choctaws kept the French settlers alive.

Two years later, the French government made New Orleans, at the mouth of the Mississippi River, the capital of Louisiana. Mobile remained a major center for the fur trade, but as New Orleans grew, Mobile declined in commercial importance.

By this time, the French had a competitor for the profitable fur trade in the Mississippi River Valley: Britain. British traders and their Native American allies claimed a growing share of the trade, despite French efforts to keep them out of the region.

This rivalry was one of the causes of the French and Indian War in North America. The war ended with France's defeat, and in the peace settlement that followed, France had to give up its lands east of the Mississippi River to Britain.

This sketch shows Mobile as it looked in 1711, the year Jean-Baptiste Le Moyne, Sieur de Bienville, moved the settlement to the shores of Mobile Bay. The flag flying from the fort (left side) features the symbol of France.

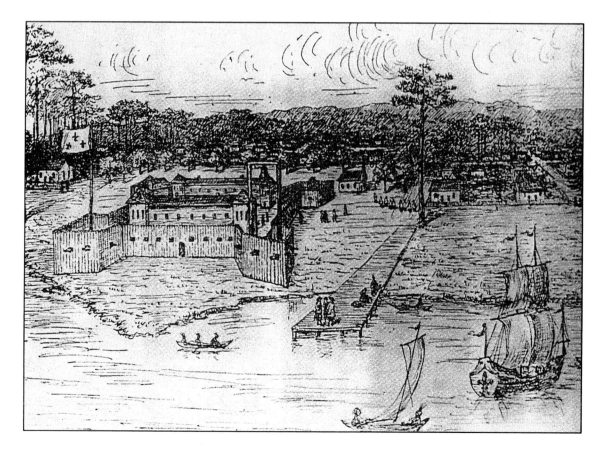

Alabama Becomes American

The British flag flew over Alabama for just seventeen years. During that time, British colonists established a few farming settlements along the region's rivers, but Alabama's interior was left mostly to the Native Americans and the traders who lived among them.

Mobile was the region's only important town, although its population, which was about 6,000 during the heyday of the French era, had fallen to a few hundred people by the mid-1700s. Mobile still kept much of its French character, but it was now home to a varied population that included, in a visitor's words, "French gentlemen, English, Scotch, and Irish, and immigrants from the Northern British Colonies," plus many African-American slaves.

During the Revolutionary War, Mobile also became a haven for Loyalists—American colonists who didn't support the movement for independence from Britain.

In 1780, Spain briefly regained control of Mobile. That nation had entered the war on the side of the rebellious American colonists, and during that time Spanish troops from New Orleans captured the city.

The Treaty of Paris, signed in 1783, ended the Revolutionary War. Under its terms, the western border of the new United States of America was set at the Mississippi River. This placed most of present-day Alabama on American soil, but a strip of land along the Gulf of Mexico—including Mobile—remained under Spanish rule.

Northern Alabama was at first claimed by Georgia, but in 1798 the region became part of the Mississippi Territory, which extended from the Chattahoochee River (which now forms part of the border between the two states) to the Mississippi River.

Two years later, France forced Spain to give up almost all of its remaining territory in North America. In 1803 France sold this vast land to the United States in the famous Louisiana Purchase. American officials believed that the purchase included Mobile, but Spain refused to give up its claim to the city.

Meanwhile, conflict was brewing between the United States and Great Britain. When war finally came in 1812, it brought crisis to Alabama's Native Americans.

Some groups, including the Choctaws, sided with the Americans against the British. Others, including many tribes of the Creek Confederacy, supported the British. Some groups, like the Muskogee branch of the Creeks, were divided over which side to support.

The pro-British Creeks hoped a British victory would keep land-hungry American settlers out of their homelands. They were inspired by Tecumseh, one of the greatest Native American leaders, who had traveled from the Great Lakes to Florida in a campaign to unite Native Americans against the United States. Tecumseh gave bundles of red twigs to chiefs of tribes who agreed to fight the Americans, so the pro-British Creeks were known as Red Sticks.

Fighting between the Red Sticks and American settlers began with a battle at Burnt Corn Creek, near the present-day town of Belleville, Alabama, in July 1813. The Red Sticks forced the Americans to retreat. Panicked settlers soon crowded into a crude fort at Samuel Mims's farm.

On August 30, more than 700 Creeks attacked Fort Mims. In a battle that lasted from noon to nightfall, most of the white settlers were killed, including many women and children.

News of the Fort Mims Massacre spread like wildfire along the frontier. Hundreds of settlers volunteered to fight the Red Sticks.

When word of the massacre reached Tennessee, the legislature quickly organized 3,500 troops and

This engraving depicts a dramatic but not very realistic view of the attack on Fort Mims on August 30, 1813. The massacre might not have happened if the fort's commander had posted guards outside its walls. Pro-British Red Sticks achieved total surprise over the 100 U.S. soldiers and 400 civilians inside.

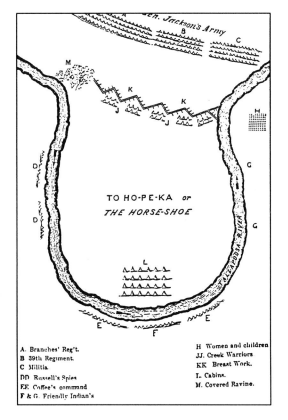

A. Branches' Reg't.
B 39th Regiment.
C Militia.
DD Russell's Spies
FF Coffee's command
F & G Friendly Indian's

H Women and children
JJ. Creek Warriors
KK Breast Work.
L. Cabins.
M. Covered Ravine.

elected Andrew Jackson, a tough lawyer and soldier, to lead the attack against the Creeks. Only weeks before the massacre, Jackson had been severely wounded in a duel, and when he received his assignment he was still too weak to get out of bed. Nevertheless, nine days later Jackson and his frontier army left Tennessee. They blazed a trail of destruction through Alabama, attacking the Red Sticks wherever they found them and burning many Native American villages—including some that didn't support the Red Sticks.

The climax of the Creek War came on March 27, 1814, at Horseshoe Bend, where the Tallapoosa River curves in on itself. Jackson, 1,500 soldiers, and 600 pro-U.S. Native Americans fought 1,000 Red Sticks led by Chief Menawa. Jackson's men stormed the log barriers the Red Sticks had thrown up while the

Jackson's opponent at the Battle of Horseshoe Bend was Menawa (top), a Creek chief who had long resisted white settlement in Alabama. Later, he helped the U.S. Army in its fight against the Seminoles in Florida in return for a promise that he would be allowed to return to his own land. The government broke its promise, and Menawa was banished to Indian Territory, where he died in 1835.

Shown left is Jackson's battle plan against the Creeks. Although the curve in the Tallapoosa River protected the Creeks on three sides, they could not hold back the militia made up of American troops and pro-U.S. Indians. Upon defeat, the Creeks were forced to hand over 20 million acres of land to the United States.

pro-U.S. Indians destroyed the Red Sticks' canoes, cutting off any hope of escape. When the four-hour fight was over, some 800 Red Sticks were dead. Jackson and his Native American allies lost fewer than fifty men.

The American victory at Horseshoe Bend crushed the Red Sticks and broke the power of the Creek Confederacy. A few months later, Jackson forced the Creek leaders, even those who had not fought against the United States, to sign away their lands in Alabama.

By this time, American troops had also seized Mobile from Spain. Thus, when the war of 1812 ended, all of present-day Alabama was under American control.

Congress officially organized the Territory of Alabama in March 1817. So many settlers arrived in the territory that fewer than two years later Alabama met the population requirement to apply for statehood. On December 14, 1819, Alabama was admitted to the Union as the twenty-second state.

William Weatherford, known as Chief Red Eagle, was only one-eighth Creek, yet he led the Indians in the attack against settlers at Fort Mims. After the Battle of Horseshoe Bend, Weatherford visited Jackson's tent to personally surrender. Jackson, impressed by the chief's courage, set him free with a warning to never again attack U.S. troops. Weatherford lived out the rest of his life as a farmer.

The Cotton Kingdom

The first four decades of Alabama's statehood was an era of fantastic growth. In 1813, at the start of the Creek War, perhaps 12,000 whites and African-American slaves lived in Alabama. By 1819, the year Alabama became a state, its population stood at about 130,000. Forty years later, in 1860, the population approached the 1 million mark.

The reasons for this growth can be summed up in one word: cotton. The crop had been grown in the South since colonial times, but it wasn't particularly profitable.

Bales of cotton slide down a chute to a waiting steamboat on the Alabama River in this engraving. In the decades before the Civil War, Alabama produced one-fourth of all the cotton harvested in the United States.

Then, in 1793, a Connecticut inventor named Eli Whitney invented the cotton gin. This machine ("gin" is short for the word engine) gave planters a fast, easy way to separate the cotton fiber from the seed. Alabama's first cotton gin was set up by Abraham Mordecai, a Jewish settler, in 1802.

The rise in cotton production came at the same time as the Industrial Revolution swept Britain and the northern United States. Water and

steam-powered mills sprang up to spin cotton into cloth. Cotton quickly became the South's most valuable crop.

The coming of the cotton gin also strengthened slavery in the South. Before the rise of the "Cotton Kingdom," many Southerners had hoped slavery would die out. But most planters came to depend on inexpensive slave labor to boost their cotton profits.

Because the soil of "Upper South" states like Virginia was worn out from centuries of tobacco planting, "Deep South" states like Georgia, Mississippi, and Alabama became the leading producers of cotton—known as white gold. In Alabama, cotton cultivation

Mobile's importance as a port is evident in this 19th-century painting, which shows Mobile Bay crammed with ships. After arriving at the port by way of the Alabama and Tombigbee rivers, cotton from inland Alabama was shipped to mills in New England and Europe.

was centered in the Black Belt, a rich band of soil extending through the central part of the state.

Thousands of newcomers arrived in Alabama in the 1820s and 1830s to cash in on the cotton boom. Usually they traveled to Mobile by ship and then up the Alabama and Tombigbee rivers by steamboat into the cotton country. Some were wealthy planters from the Upper South, bringing hundreds of slaves with them to work their new plantations. Others came with a slave or two, or on their own, hoping that hard work would pay off.

In the first half of the 19th century, settlers from Kentucky, Tennessee, and northern Georgia also began to arrive in the mountain and plateau region of northern Alabama. These settlers had little in common with the cotton planters of the Black Belt. They built their homes on hilly, forested land with sandy soil that would not grow cotton. It took backbreaking effort just to grow enough corn and vegetables to survive. The farmers of northern Alabama resented the wealth of the plantation society in the Black Belt, and the political power the planters held in the state government.

But white Alabamians of all kinds had one thing in common: A desire to seize the lands belonging to the state's remaining Native Americans.

Unlike most other Native American nations, the Cherokees, Choctaws, and Chickasaws of Alabama adapted well to the white way of life. Many became Christians, married into white families, and ran successful farms and plantations. Some even owned slaves. These Native Americans were *too* successful in the eyes of the many white settlers who wanted their land.

In 1830, the Choctaws were pressured into signing a one-sided treaty giving up their territory in Alabama and agreeing to move to Indian Territory (now Oklahoma) across the Mississippi River. They left the state in

1831 and were followed a few years later by the Chickasaws.

The Creeks also agreed to "removal," but some resisted when whites broke the terms of the removal treaty. In the end, however, they too left their fertile homeland for the dry plains of Indian Territory.

Many Native Americans and some whites protested this unfair treatment, and their case went all the way to the Supreme Court. The court actually overruled a federal law that had set the stage for Indian removal, but the old Indian fighter Andrew Jackson—now president of the United States—refused to enforce the court's decision.

The last and most widespread removal came in 1838, when thousands of Cherokees were rounded up by the U.S. Army and herded to Indian Territory at gunpoint. As many as 4,000 Cherokees died of hunger, disease, and cold along the way. In addition, the Indians were often attacked and robbed by bands of settlers who felt that the Native Americans owed them some imaginary debt.

The Cherokees called the route to Indian Territory the Trail of Tears.

In 1838, the U.S. government forced thousands of Cherokees to move from their homes in Alabama and Georgia to Indian Territory in order to make room for white settlers in the region. About one out of every four Cherokees died during or shortly after the 800-mile journey, which came to be known as the Trail of Tears.

Cradle of the Confederacy

Montgomery, in central Alabama, was the state's first capital, but in 1820 the state government moved to Cahaba, in the southern part of the state. Low-lying Cahaba was prone to flooding, however, and in 1826 the capital was moved again, this time to Tuscaloosa. Finally, in 1846, Montgomery again became the state's capital, and remains so today.

Alabama's output of cotton doubled every ten years during the first half of the 19th century. As in the rest of the Cotton Kingdom of the South, this would have been im-possible without the labor provided by slaves. By 1860, the national census showed that there were almost as many slaves as white people in the state—435,000 to about 525,000, respectively—and that 10 percent of all the slaves in the country lived in Alabama.

Still, the Hollywood image of slavery in the Deep South—huge plantations worked by hundreds

Montgomery was one of the largest slave markets in the South. Here, two slaves stand on the auction block while the auctioneer takes bids. Entire families were often broken up and sold to separate owners, an aspect of slavery that especially outraged many people in the non-slave states.

of slaves—wasn't the case in Alabama. Most cotton planters owned fewer than five slaves, and only about forty plantation owners in the entire state owned more than 200 slaves.

Slavery was the greatest controversy facing the United States in the mid-1800s. Many people in the Northern states, where slavery was outlawed, had no quarrel with slavery in the South—although a small but growing group of men and women, known as abolitionists, called for a total ban on slavery. Most northerners, however, didn't want to see slavery spread to the new states and territories west of the Mississippi River.

Most white Alabamians supported slavery. Even if fewer than one in three Alabamians owned slaves, slave-grown cotton was the mainstay of the entire region's economy.

William Lowndes Yancey was one of slavery's staunchest defenders. Born in Georgia and raised in New York, Yancey came to Alabama, became a planter, served a term in Congress, and then made a career of writing and speaking in favor of slavery. Yancey's argument—that slavery was a "positive good," not just for the South, but for the entire nation—found favor with many white Alabamians.

Political compromises kept the peace between the free and slave states for decades, but the election of 1860 put the nation on the brink of civil war. Abraham Lincoln, candi-date of the antislavery Republican Party, won the election. Unwilling to accept Lincoln's leadership, Southern states began to secede (withdraw) from the Union.

In January 1861, a statewide convention met at Montgomery and voted to secede. The document declaring Alabama's secession was drafted by William Lowndes Yancey.

A month later, representatives from the seceded states gathered at Mont-

William Lowndes Yancey was one of the most impassioned champions of slavery. During the 1840s, Yancey opposed Northern attempts to forbid slavery in the Western territories, a policy some called the Alabama Platform. Yancey later served the Confederate government as a diplomat in Europe.

gomery to organize a new nation—the Confederate States of America. As crowds cheered wildly, Jefferson Davis of Mississippi was sworn in as the Confederacy's first president on February 16.

Montgomery served as the Confederacy's capital only until May 1861, when Davis moved his government to Richmond, Virginia. Still, the city is often called the Cradle of the Confederacy for the role it played in the Confederacy's first days.

Not all Alabamians cheered the events in Montgomery. In the hill country of northeastern Alabama, the mostly antislavery population bitterly opposed secession. One county even seceded from Alabama as the "Free State of Winston."

When war between the Confederacy and the Union (non-seceded states) broke out in 1861, many men in the region refused orders to serve in the Confederate Army and went into hiding in the rugged countryside. Some 3,000 others left the state to serve in the Union Army. Another 10,000 slaves escaped and joined the Union forces during the course of the war.

"The man and the hour have met!" proclaimed William Lowndes Yancey on February 16, 1861, when Jefferson Davis, the newly elected president of the Confederate States of America, arrived in Montgomery. Two days later, Davis was sworn in as president as depicted in this print, which is based on a photograph of the scene.

More than 120,000 Alabama men fought for the Confederacy, and many died in combat or of disease in four long years of war. In one regiment, only about 250 out of 1,200 men survived to return home to Alabama.

Union forces occupied a few northern Alabama towns, including Tuscumbia and Decatur, and in 1862 and again in 1863 Union cavalry tried unsuccessfully to cross the state and raid Atlanta, Georgia. Until 1864, however, Alabama escaped the fighting that ravaged much of the South.

In that year, the Union launched a naval campaign aimed at closing the port of Mobile. President Lincoln had ordered the Southern coast blockaded (sealed off) to keep weapons and other supplies from overseas from reaching the Confederacy. New Orleans and other port cities had fallen to the Union by 1864, but Mobile remained in Confederate hands.

In August, Union admiral David Farragut led an eighteen-ship fleet into Mobile Bay. Guarding the harbor were two forts, a few small Confederate warships, and many underwater mines, or torpedoes, as they were then called.

Farragut's lead ship, the *Tecumseh*, hit a torpedo, blew up, and sank. The rest of the Union vessels halted, but Farragut ordered them forward into the bay with a battle cry that soon became famous: "Damn the torpedoes! Full speed ahead!"

Farragut's fleet steamed into the bay and, after an hour of furious fighting, blocked the Confederates from entering the port of Mobile. (The city itself wasn't captured until a year later, in the closing days of war.) The Battle of Mobile Bay was one of the most important naval battles of the Civil War.

By the spring of 1865 the Confederacy was on the edge of defeat. The last major fighting in Alabama came early in April, when 13,000 Union cavalrymen raided Selma, the site of one of the dying Confederacy's last weapons plants.

Selma was still burning on April 9 when, in far-off Virginia, Confederate commanding general Robert E. Lee surrendered. The few Confederate troops left in Alabama surrendered a month later. Like the rest of the South, Alabama suffered heavy losses during the Civil War. The parts of the state that had seen the most fighting were devastated. Homes and businesses had been burned; railroads were torn up and destroyed; once-thriving plantations lay in ruins.

Hunger, disease, and lawlessness spread. Alabama's people, both white and African American, looked toward an uncertain future.

Admiral Farragut's Union fleet steams into Mobile Bay in this painting of the great Civil War battle. The vessel in the lower left foreground is the ironclad *Tennessee*, one of the last major warships in the Confederate Navy. Farragut's gunners disabled the *Tennessee* in a high point of the fight.

TIMES OF STRUGGLE, TIMES OF CHANGE

Iron ore, coal, and limestone—the three necessary components in iron production—were all found in abundance in the northern region of Alabama, making it the ideal place to base the South's iron industry. Between 1885 and 1892, the state's annual iron production jumped from 203,000 to 915,000 tons per year.

In the years following the Civil War, white backlash against newly freed slaves kept Alabama's African Americans from taking their place as full citizens, and a system of sharecropping kept many tied to the land. At the same time, the state's economy revived as industry, especially iron, developed in northern Alabama. In the 20th century, Alabama struggled through the Depression and played a major role in launching the space age. Alabama was a major battleground in the civil rights movement of the 1950s and 1960s, and thanks to the brave men and women who often risked their lives in the cause, the state's African Americans finally began to enjoy their rights as citizens.

Reconstruction and Revival

The end of the war brought freedom for Alabama's 500,000 slaves. During Reconstruction, which is the name for the decade following the war, Alabama's newly freed African Americans began to enjoy some of the political and civil rights guaranteed to all Americans by the Constitution. But this period didn't last very long. Many white Alabamians fought all efforts to achieve equality between the races.

Not long after the war's end, the Alabama legislature passed several laws known together as the "black codes." These laws restricted the freedom of blacks by, among other things, forbidding them to travel and by forcing them to work. The legislature also refused to ratify (approve) the Fourteenth Amendment to the Constitution, which guaranteed some basic civil rights to African Americans.

The federal government responded by putting Alabama under military rule. The legislature was now run by carpetbaggers—Northern politicians who went south after the war—and white Alabamians who had opposed the state's secession from the Union before the war. In addition, many ex-Confederate Alabamians were forbidden to vote, which made it very easy for the new state government to approve a constitution that guaranteed civil rights to African-American men.

By the early 1870s, three African Americans had been elected to represent Alabama in Congress.

But military rule and "carpetbagger government" only increased the anger and bitterness of many of the state's whites. Some turned to violence. In the early 1870s, groups like the Ku Klux Klan operated in Alabama, terrorizing and sometimes killing African Americans who dared to exercise their newly-won rights.

As white resistance rose, Northern interest in Reconstruction fell. By 1874, when the last federal troops left the ex-Confederate states, the federal government and the rest of the country decided to leave the South alone. For African Americans in Alabama and elsewhere, this meant the loss of both the political and civil rights they had so briefly enjoyed.

After the war, some African Americans remained on the plantations, working on the land in return for wages. But soon a new system, called sharecropping, developed. In this system, African-American families grew cotton on small plots of white-owned land. The sharecropper was entitled to a portion of the money earned from the sale of the cotton. From this money, however, the sharecropper had to pay the landowner for food, tools, and other necessities.

This engraving shows Alabamians waiting to receive food rations in an office of the Freedmen's Bureau. The bureau, a federal agency set up to help ex-slaves make the transition to freedom, also helped poor whites in the desperate years following the end of the Civil War.

As a result—and because some landowners took every opportunity to cheat their tenants—a sharecropping family might work the whole year only to find themselves actually owing money to the landowner. This debt would be carried on to the next generation, and then the next, trapping sharecroppers in a system that many considered just as bad, or even worse, than slavery.

But even as sharecropping took hold in the state, Alabama took the lead in bringing industry to the mostly agricultural South.

The center of this Southern industrial growth was the Jones Valley in the northern part of the state. For decades people had known that the region contained plentiful deposits of iron ore, coal, and limestone—all needed for making iron—but little had been done to tap these resources until the Civil War.

During the conflict, iron from the area was used to make ammunition and weapons for the Confederacy. After the war, some farsighted Alabamians realized the Jones Valley was perfectly suited to the production of iron and steel.

In 1870, two railroads laid track into the valley. A year later, a new town was founded at the point where the tracks joined. The town's founders named it Birmingham, after a great industrial city in England.

In its first years, the new town suffered an epidemic of the deadly disease cholera and weathered a nationwide economic depression. But after 1880, when the first steel-producing blast furnace opened for business, Birmingham enjoyed a spectacular economic boom. By 1890, Birmingham's population had risen from about 3,000 to nearly 30,000. With its steel mills belching smoke and flame night and day, Birmingham

A symbol of Alabama's newfound industrial muscle was the Mary Pratt Furnace, a blast furnace built in Birmingham in 1882. Its owner, Henry DeBardeleben, was the son-in-law of early Alabama industrialist Daniel Pratt. He named the furnace after his daughter, Mary Pratt DeBardeleben.

soon won the nickname "the Pittsburgh of the South."

In the last decades of the century, Alabama also increased educational opportunities for African Americans and women.

In 1881, a young ex-slave from Virginia, Booker T. Washington, arrived in Alabama. Outside Montgomery, Washington founded Tuskegee Institute, a school devoted to teaching important skills to African-American students and to training teachers for African-American communities.

Tuskegee soon became one of the nation's most important African-American educational institutions, and Booker T. Washington became the nation's most influential African-American leader.

In 1896, Washington brought the

In keeping with Booker T. Washington's belief that economic progress was the most important goal for African Americans, Tuskegee Institute taught both practical subjects like farming and building and academic subjects like literature and chemistry. Here, students are shown at work in the institute's laboratory.

African-American scientist George Washington Carver to Tuskegee to serve as the institute's director of agricultural research—a post Carver held for nearly fifty years. In the course of his amazing career, Carver developed hundreds of uses for common crops like peanuts and sweet potatoes, which increased the value of Southern agriculture.

While Washington and Carver were transforming African-American education at Tuskegee, Julia Tutwiler worked to expand educational oppor-

tunities for women in the state. After the Civil War, Tutwiler ran the Alabama Normal College, which trained young women to serve as teachers. In the 1890s, Tutwiler led a long and eventually successful fight to allow women to attend the University of Alabama.

Another important Alabama woman who won fame at this time was Tuscumbia-born Helen Keller. A childhood disease robbed Keller of her sight and hearing at the age of nineteen months. Her family believed she would be trapped forever in a sightless, soundless world, but with the help of a remarkable teacher, Anne Sullivan, Keller learned to communicate when she was only seven years old.

For the rest of her long life Helen Keller worked tirelessly as an educator, writer, and supporter of many social reforms. She earned the world's admiration and forever changed the way people look at the disabled.

Much of George Washington Carver's (top) pioneering work at Tuskegee Institute, including his famous experiments with soybeans, sweet potatoes, and, especially peanuts, came from his desire to improve the lives of Alabama's desperately poor sharecroppers.

Although blind and deaf, Helen Keller (left) graduated from Radcliffe College in Cambridge, Massachusetts, with honors in 1904. She went on to write eleven books, including her autobiography, and dedicated her life to educating people about blindness and disabilities. She died in 1968.

Into the 20th Century

Alabama entered the 20th century with a population of more than 1.5 million. Despite the growth of industry in the years since the Civil War, the state remained largely rural: Nearly nine out of every ten Alabamians lived and worked on the land. Many of Alabama's African Americans remained tied to the land as sharecroppers, and over the years the sharecropping system grew to include many of the state's poorer whites.

With the coming of the new century, the African-American struggle for equality took a huge step backward.

After Reconstruction ended, the state government, now completely dominated by whites, had passed laws aimed at keeping African Americans and whites segregated—separated—on trains, in restaurants and theaters, and in almost all other public places. In 1896, the U.S. Supreme Court had approved segregation as long as facilities for both races were "separate but equal." In practice, they rarely were. The segregation system made Alabama's African Americans second-class citizens in their own state.

Sharecroppers chop cotton in this photograph. It took the hard work of all family members for sharecroppers to survive, which often meant that children did not have the time or opportunity to get an education. Without the ability to read or write, most of them remained tied to the land as adults.

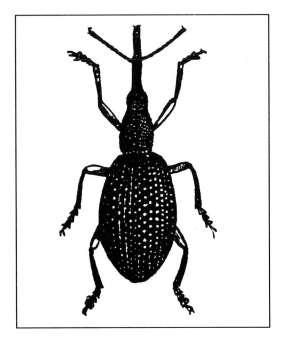

Cotton lies baled and ready for shipment in Montgomery in this turn-of-the-century postcard (above). The rapid growth of textile mills in Alabama in the first decades of the 20th century meant that much cotton now stayed in the state, instead of being shipped to other parts of the country or overseas for processing into cloth.

The boll weevil (left), scientifically known as *Anthonomus grandis*, came to Alabama in 1913 from Mexico by way of Texas. The growing larvae (young) of the beetle eats away at the boll (bloom) of the cotton plant. If left unchecked, it can destroy entire cotton harvests.

Despite the rise of segregation, some brave African-American Alabamians had continued to vote in the decades following the Civil War. That changed after 1901, when a new state constitution was adopted. The 1901 constitution introduced a number of obstacles, including a poll tax and literacy tests, aimed at keeping African Americans (and poor whites) away from the polls. It worked: Between 1901 and 1951, only about 5 percent of the state's eligible African-American voters were able to cast a ballot in any given election.

The first decades of the new century brought changes to Alabama's economy. Production of cotton, the state's most important product for almost a century, began to fall after 1910. In that year, the boll weevil, a cotton-eating insect from Mexico, began to spread across the state.

But the boll weevil plague turned out to be a blessing in disguise: By ruining cotton harvests, the weevil forced farmers to plant new crops, including peanuts, which greatly expanded Alabama's agricultural base. The town of Enterprise even built a monument to the insect "in appreciation of what it has done to herald prosperity."

Still, cotton remained vital to Alabama in more ways than one. In the early 1900s, textile mills, which processed cotton into cloth, sprang up in Huntsville and other cities.

Many were built by Northern textile companies attracted by the state's low labor costs: The mills paid low wages, but to many poor Alabamians life as a millworker was better than life as a sharecropper.

Mill machinery was often operated by children, some as young as ten years old, who worked twelve-hour days for as little as 15 cents a day. In 1915, however, the state legislature passed laws restricting child labor.

Alabama's steel industry continued to expand, especially after 1907, when the giant U.S. Steel Corporation built a plant in Birmingham. U.S. Steel and other manufacturers often used convicts from state prisons to work in their mines. Many Alabamians opposed the practice, but it wasn't until 1928 that reformers managed to end the practice.

America's entry into World War I brought Alabama a measure of prosperity that lasted into the 1920s. Steel plants and textile mills worked night and day to fill military orders; Mobile's shipyards turned out scores of warships and merchant vessels; and the state's farmers benefited from a rise in demand for cotton and food crops.

The coming of the war also led to a huge federal project in Alabama: The construction of a dam across the Tennessee River. The dam, which was eventually named for then-president Woodrow Wilson, was built to serve two purposes. First, it would supply

electricity for plants producing nitrate, a chemical used to make explosives. Second, it would flood a forty-mile stretch of shallow, rock-filled water known as Muscle Shoals, making it possible for ships to navigate the Tennessee River up to and into the Ohio River.

The ambitious project wasn't completed until 1924—six years after the war's end. Federal and state officials argued for years about what to do with the dam. In the meantime, plants that had been built to make nitrate for bombs and shells began turning it out for use as fertilizer.

Recruiters pose outside their Birmingham office during World War I. Some 86,000 Alabamians served in the U.S. armed forces during the conflict; among the 6,000 Alabamians who lost their lives was Osmond Kelly Ingram of the U.S. Navy, the first American sailor to die in combat in World War I.

From the TVA to the Space Age

Alabamians endured great hardships in the Depression years of the 1930s. The economic slump hit both rural and industrial Alabama hard. Steel plants, textile mills, factories, and other businesses slowed or closed altogether, putting tens of thousands of Alabamians out of work.

Cotton, which sold in the early 1920s for about 40 cents a pound, dropped to a nickel or less a pound a decade later. The steep drop drove many cotton planters out of business, forcing sharecropping families into homelessness. An Alabama congressman reported in 1932, "My people are desperate. They are in an agony of starvation and ruin. . . ."

Help came from the federal government in the form of President Franklin Roosevelt's New Deal programs. The Farm Security Administration (FSA), for example, provided food, seeds, and tools to poor farming families. Some 70,000 Alabamians found employment with the Civilian Conservation Corps (CCC) and Works Progress Administration (WPA). These agencies put people to work on projects such as building roads and parks, and caring for forests.

Shown here is a homeless child outside a trailer on the outskirts of Birmingham—a common sight in the Depression-ravaged Alabama of the 1930s, a time when few were spared hardship.

The greatest public-works program in Alabama was the Tennessee Valley Authority (TVA). Begun in 1933, this vast project was aimed at improving the lives of the nearly 3 million Alabamians who lived in the valley of the Tennessee River, which snakes across northern Alabama.

The TVA's main goal was the construction of two new dams across the river, in addition to the already completed Wilson Dam at Muscle Shoals. The project's supporters, including future Alabama senator Lister Hill, outlined the benefits the dams would bring: flood control, improved navigation on the river, and clean water and inexpensive electricity for the valley's poverty-stricken people.

The dams, completed in the late 1930s, fulfilled the TVA's promise. Thanks to the Rural Electrification Administration (REA), which controlled the electricity generated by the dams, the valley's people had affordable power for their homes and farms.

World War II pulled Alabama out of the Depression. Between 1941 and 1945, the state's factories filled half a billion dollars' worth of wartime orders. Alabamians who had known lives of grinding poverty as sharecroppers now found they could make good money working in defense plants. This helped to break down the old sharecropping system, which had never recovered from the effects of the Depression.

The war also sped up the move of people from the countryside to Alabama's cities. By the war's end, some 300,000 rural Alabamians had moved to Birmingham, Mobile, Huntsville, and other cities.

Because Alabama's warm climate allows year-round military training, many important bases, training camps, and airfields were set up in Alabama. One of these, Tuskegee Army Air Field, trained African-American pilots for the Army Air Corps, as the Air Force was called at the time. About 1,000 pilots, known as the Tuskegee Airmen, trained at the facility.

At the war's end, a number of German scientists, veterans of the German military's rocket program, surrendered to the American forces. They were brought to the United States along with their leader, Dr. Wehrner von Braun, to help the United States develop its own rockets.

The group was based in Texas at first, but in 1950 the U.S. rocket program moved to Redstone Arsenal (the

A worker tends a phosphate-smelting furnace at the TVA chemical plant at Muscle Shoals in this 1942 photograph (opposite, top). Thanks to the power provided by the TVA, Alabama was a major supplier of war materials during the conflict.

In this photograph (right), African-American trainee pilots, known as the Tuskegee Airmen, study navigation at Tuskegee Army Air Field under the guidance of a white instructor. (The U.S. military was segregated at the time, and there were relatively few black officers.)

former Redstone Ordnance Plant) in Huntsville.

Over the next decade, von Braun and his fellow scientists laid the foundation of the U.S. space program. In the process they turned the small town into "Rocket City, USA," as research laboratories, launch pads, and assembly plants were built in and around Huntsville. The facilities drew engineers and scientists from around the nation.

The Huntsville team scored its first success with the launch of the *Redstone* rocket in 1953. Two years later, an even more powerful rocket, the *Jupiter*, soared into the skies over Huntsville.

In 1957, the Soviet Union launched *Sputnik*, the world's first satellite. Worried that the United States was now behind in the "space race," von Braun and his scientists went into high gear to put an American satellite into space. In February 1958, they succeeded: A *Jupiter* rocket blasted into space carrying the *Explorer I* satellite into orbit.

Later that year, Congress organized the National Aeronautics and Space Administration (NASA) to coordinate the nation's space program. Two years later, NASA built its first headquarters, the George C. Marshall Space Center, at Huntsville.

This massive *Saturn* rocket was developed by Wehrner von Braun and his associates at Huntsville. Once a town best known for exporting watercress, Huntsville's population swelled from 15,000 in 1945 to about 125,000 just two decades later as the "space race" heated up.

The Civil Rights Revolution

As America reached into space, a revolution of another kind gathered strength in Alabama. This was the civil rights movement—a struggle to end the hated system of segregation, to break down the barriers that kept African Americans from voting and participating in politics, and to restore the rights that were denied to African Americans in Alabama and other Southern states.

Events in the 1930s and 1940s helped set the stage. The long legal battle to free the "Scottsboro Boys," a group of young African-American men wrongly accused of raping two white women, made Americans aware that it was nearly impossible for African Americans to get a fair trial in an Alabama court.

During World War II, some Alabamians protested the segregated training given to African-American pilots at Tuskegee. And when African-American soldiers returned home to Alabama after the war, they brought with them a new sense of the unfairness of segregation. "After having been overseas fighting for democracy," one veteran later said, "I thought that when we got back here we should enjoy a little of it."

Most of the state's white citizens either supported segregation or felt the system was impossible to change. Some did speak out in favor of civil

Born in Atlanta, Georgia, Martin Luther King, Jr., attended Morehouse College, Crozier Theological Seminary, and Boston University before becoming pastor of Montgomery's Dexter Avenue Baptist Church in 1955. King was honored with a Nobel Peace Prize in 1964 for his tireless and effective leadership in the civil rights cause.

rights, but it was an unpopular stand. In 1951, for example, Governor Jim Folsom was attacked by fellow politicians for stating that "too many [African Americans] have maliciously been denied the right to vote . . . that is not democracy in any sense."

The U.S. Supreme Court struck a major blow against segregation in the 1954 *Brown* v. *Board of Education* decision, which declared segregation in public schools unconstitutional. But Alabama's schools remained segregated, along with movie theaters, restaurants, and other public gathering places.

Public transportation, too, was segregated. In Montgomery, African Americans riding city buses were required to give up their seats to white passengers. But on December 1,

1955, an African-American woman, Rosa Parks, tired after a long day of work, refused to move to the back of the bus to make way for a white rider. She was arrested.

Parks's plight inspired a young Baptist minister, Martin Luther King, Jr., to lead the African-American community in a challenge against the segregated bus system. King, a student of the writings and actions of figures like Henry David Thoreau and Mahatma Ghandi, had come to believe that campaigns of peaceful, nonviolent

A U.S. Justice Department official confronts Governor George Wallace (in doorway) during the June 1963 crisis over desegregation at the University of Alabama. After Wallace backed down, two African-American students were finally allowed to enter the university.

protest were the right way to fight segregation.

Under King's leadership, Montgomery's African-American citizens began a boycott of the buses: They refused to ride until the system was desegregated, even though this meant much hardship and inconvenience.

The boycott lasted more than a year, but the buses were finally integrated. This stunning victory brought King to the forefront of the growing civil rights movement.

Segregation's supporters found their champion in George Wallace, a young politician who believed that the federal government's support for civil rights and desegregation violated Alabama's rights as a state. At his inaugural in 1963, Wallace proclaimed, "Segregation now, segregation tomorrow, segregation forever. . . ."

While the governor defied the federal government, other pro-segregation Alabamians took the law into their own hands. When African Americans marched in Birmingham to protest segregation in stores and restaurants, the city's police commissioner, Eugene "Bull" Conner, turned fire hoses and attack dogs on the peaceful marchers.

Later that year, Wallace personally barred the door when two African-American students tried to register at the University of Alabama in Tuscaloosa. The fiery governor finally allowed the students to enter after a federal official arrived with National Guard troops.

In September, a bomb exploded in Birmingham's Sixteenth Street Baptist Church, killing four young African-American girls. A member of the Ku Klux Klan was later found guilty of setting the bomb.

The events of 1963 were tragic, but they were also a turning point in the movement against segregation. Televised images of the violence in Birmingham convinced many Americans of the justice of the civil rights cause, and support for integration grew.

The following year, Congress passed the landmark Civil Rights Act of 1964, which overturned the entire system of segregation. It would be a long time before all the new law's provisions were enforced in Alabama and other Southern states, but the wall that separated whites and African Americans finally began to fall.

After the passage of the Civil Rights Act, King and other civil rights leaders turned their energies to securing voting rights.

In February 1965, hundreds of African Americans tried to register to vote in Selma. When all but a handful were turned away from the Dallas County courthouse, Martin Luther King, Jr., vowed to lead a protest march from Selma to the state capitol at Montgomery. The protesters had

barely left Selma's city limits on March 7, however, before state and local police broke up the march with tear gas and clubs.

King was not discouraged: He announced another march. Civil rights supporters of all races poured into Selma from across the country. On March 21, King and 3,000 marchers again left Selma for the fifty-mile journey to Montgomery. This time President Johnson, angered at the treatment the protesters had received during their first march, ordered the United States Army to protect them from angry police.

After five days on the road, the weary but joyful marchers, now numbering more than 25,000, arrived in Montgomery. Standing near the spot where George Wallace had given his "Segregation forever!" speech, King proclaimed, "We are on the move now. . . . Let us march on to the realization of the American dream."

In August 1965, President Johnson signed the Voting Rights of 1965 into law. The act outlawed the old system of poll taxes, property qualifications, and other obstacles that kept African Americans from voting.

With the fall of segregation and the establishment of voting rights, Alabama, and all the South, began a new era. But Martin Luther King, Jr., would not live to see the seeds of freedom bear fruit. He lost his life to an assassin's bullet in Memphis, Tennessee, in April 1968.

African Americans line up to vote in Peachtree in 1966 (above), one year after the passage of the Voting Rights Act of 1965. This was probably the first time most of the people in this photo had ever cast a ballot.

This photograph (right) shows a woman marcher on the road from Selma to Montgomery. People of all races risked violence to end segregation and ensure civil rights for the African Americans of Alabama and the rest of the South.

Coping with Change

George Wallace continued to dominate politics in Alabama long after the segregation era began to fade into history. State law prohibited anyone from serving as governor for more than two consecutive terms, so in 1966 Wallace's wife, Lurleen Burns Wallace, was elected governor. George Wallace continued to run the state behind the scenes until Lurleen Wallace died in office in 1968.

In that same year, Wallace launched an independent run for the presidency as candidate of the American Independent Party. Wallace received more than 10 million votes, half of them from states outside the South—proof that Wallace's political influence went far beyond Alabama.

Elected governor again in 1970, Wallace returned to the Democratic Party and sought the party's nomination in the 1972 presidential election. His bid for the nomination ended in May, when Wallace was shot at a campaign rally in Maryland. The shooting left him paralyzed.

Wallace served as governor until 1979. By that time, the fiery segregationist of the 1960s had become a much more moderate politician.

As governor during the 1970s, Wallace appointed African Americans to state offices and welcomed newly registered African-American voters into the Democratic Party. Wallace claimed

Running as the presidential candidate of the American Independent Party in 1968, George Wallace and his running mate, former Air Force general Curtis LeMay, captured nearly 10 million popular votes and forty-six electoral votes—an amazing showing for a controversial third-party candidate.

that his earlier anti-segregation stand was based not on prejudice against African Americans, but on his belief that the federal government had overstepped its constitutional limits in its support for civil rights.

With the end of segregation and the establishment of voting rights, Alabama's African Americans began to enter state politics. They were helped not only by the landmark federal civil rights laws of the early 1960s, but also by a 1964 Supreme Court case, *Sims v. Reynolds.*

Before this case, representation in the state legislature was based on a system that represented some areas of the state more than others. The court declared this system unfair, and ordered reapportionment (redrawing of electoral districts) so that each Alabamian's vote counted equally.

The reformed system made it easier for African Americans to win election to local and state offices. It also gave citizens of Alabama's growing towns and cities—both white and African American—fair representation in the legislature.

Throughout the 1960s and 1970s, African-American Alabamians accomplished an impressive series of political "firsts." In 1966, Lucius Amerson was elected sheriff of Macon County—the first African American to hold such an office in the South since Reconstruction. Macon County was also the site of another important election-first six years later, when Johnny Ford

Richard Arrington's election as the first African-American mayor of Birmingham in 1979 was seen as a symbol of Alabama's progress: Only sixteen years before, blacks had had to fight for the unrestricted right to vote.

took office as mayor of Tuskegee and became the first African-American mayor of an Alabama community.

One event in particular showed how much things had changed in Alabama. In 1979, just sixteen years after police had let attack dogs loose on civil rights marchers in Birmingham's streets, an African-American politician, Richard Arrington, was elected mayor of the city.

For Alabama, the late 1960s and 1970s brought economic change, too. The steel plants in and around

Birmingham began to decline in the 1960s, when U.S. manufacturers started to buy less expensive steel from overseas. By the end of the 1970s, Alabama's once-thriving steel industry employed only a fraction of the people it had employed in the 1940s.

The movement of people from rural areas to cities and towns increased in the decades following World War II, and so did the decline in cotton's importance to Alabama's economy. Before World War II, the state had about 3.5 million acres of land planted with cotton; by the end of the 1970s, cotton acreage was less than 500,000 acres. In its place, Alabama's farmers now raise chickens and cattle; grow peanuts and soybeans; or cultivate trees for paper pulp and other wood products.

From the 1960s to the present, Birmingham, the South's "steel city," has encouraged new industries to replace jobs lost in the steel plants, which have been in decline for decades.

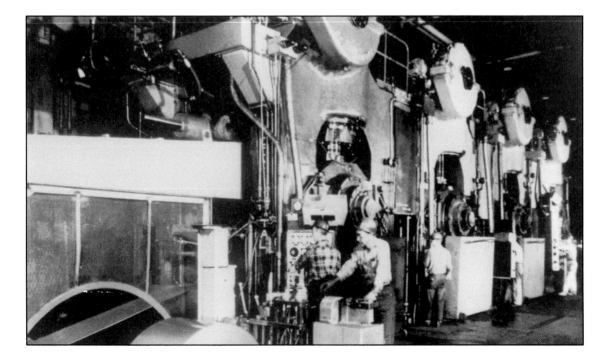

Alabama Today

Alabama began the 1980s with a population of 4 million. By the 1990s, more than six out of ten Alabamians lived in urban areas, with Birmingham, Montgomery, and Mobile remaining the state's biggest cities.

Alabama's population growth was partly due to "reverse migration." During the 1950s and 1960s, many African Americans left the state for the big cities of the Northern and Western states. When segregation ended and opportunities for African Americans opened up in Alabama, many returned.

George Wallace was elected governor again in 1983 and served until 1987. In retirement and in increasingly poor health, Wallace worked for Troy State University in Montgomery.

Although he had won his last election with the support of a majority of the state's African-American voters, and although he had appointed more African Americans to state offices than any Alabama governor, the controversial events of the early 1960s still haunted George Wallace. In a 1992 interview, a reporter quoted from Wallace's famous "segregation forever" speech. The ex-governor responded by opening his desk drawer and handing the reporter a piece of paper.

Mobile, Alabama's second-largest city, combines 19th-century charm with a bustling, modern port. Each year millions of tons of goods are shipped from Mobile to countries around the world.

It was an honorary degree from Tuskegee Institute.

Economically, Alabama has had ups and downs. The economic slump that hit the nation in the late 1970s and early 1980s was especially bad in Alabama, and for much of the 1980s the state's unemployment rate was well above the national average.

Most of the job losses occurred in heavy industries. To take up the economic slack caused by the decline in manufacturing, Alabama has turned to service industries—especially tourism. In the early 1990s, for example, Alabama sponsored the construction of seven world-class golf courses throughout the state at a cost of nearly $100 million. The state government has also worked hard to attract companies to Alabama from both the rest of the country and from overseas.

Sports is an area in which Alabamians have excelled in recent decades. Mobile native Hank Aaron made history in 1974 when he broke Babe Ruth's record to become baseball's greatest home run hitter. Paul "Bear" Bryant, coach of the University of Alabama's Crimson Tide football team, retired in 1983 after an amazing career that included twenty major bowl games and victories in five national championships. Heisman Trophy winner Bo Jackson, who began his career at Auburn University, went on to play both professional football and baseball in the 1980s and 1990s.

Few states have experienced the

"Bear" Bryant (above) was a hero to generations of University of Alabama football fans and perhaps the best-known college football coach in the history of the game.

Children and adults from all over America have attended U.S. Space Camp in Huntsville to learn about space exploration and find out what life as an astronaut would be like. Here, a Space Camp trainee tries out an MMU (manned maneuvering unit) similar to the ones used by space shuttle astronauts (opposite).

vast changes that Alabama has in the last few decades, and the state's people have done a remarkable job in adjusting to them. In many key areas—employment, education, personal income—Alabama still lags behind the rest of the country. But no state has come so far so fast in providing equal opportunities for all its citizens.

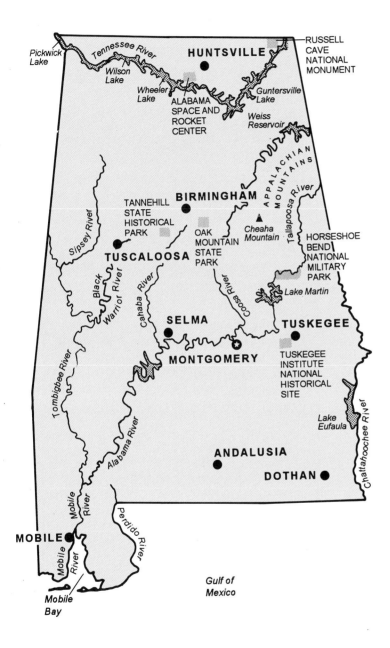

Land area:
 52,423 square miles, of which 1,673 are inland water. Ranks 29th in size.

Major rivers:
 Alabama contains more than 1,500 miles of rivers and other waterways, including the Alabama River; the Black Warrior; the Cahaba; the Chattahoochee; the Coosa; the Mobile; the Perdido; the Sipsey; the Tallapoosa; the Tennessee; the Tombigbee.

Highest point:
 Cheaha Mountain in Cleburne County, 2,405 ft.

Major bodies of water:
 The biggest lakes have all been artificially created. They include Lake Eufaula; Guntersville Lake; Lake Martin; Pickwick Lake; Weiss Reservoir; Wheeler Lake; and Wilson Lake. The state also has a short coastline on the Gulf of Mexico.

Climate:
 Average January
  temperature: 51°F
 Average July
  temperature: 82°F

Population: 4,182,00 (1993)
Rank: 22nd
    1900: 1,828,697
    1820: 127,901

Population of major cities (1992):

City	Population
Birmingham	265,965
Mobile	196,278
Montgomery	187,543
Huntsville	159,880
Tuscaloosa	77,759
Dothan	53,589

Ethnic breakdown by percentage (1993):

Group	Percentage
White	73.6%
African American	25.3%
Hispanic	0.6%
Asian	0.5%
Native American	0.4%

Economy:
Manufacturing (especially textiles, wood, and paper products); agriculture (corn, cotton, hay, hogs, peanuts, and beef cattle); shipping; tourism; and hydroelectric power.

State government:
Legislature: 35-member senate and 106-member house of representatives. Both senators and representatives serve 4-year terms.
Governor: The head of the executive branch of Alabama's government is elected for a 4-year term.
Courts: Alabama's judicial system includes the 9-judge supreme court, criminal and civil appeals courts and circuit, district, and municipal courts.
State capital: Montgomery

State Flag

Adopted in 1895, the state flag features a red Cross of St. Andrew (a diagonal cross) on a white background edged with gold. The flag has become controversial in recent years because it was inspired by the Confederate battle flag.

State Seal

Alabama's state seal is a map of the state on a gold background. The seal was officially adopted when Alabama was admitted to the Union in 1819.

State Motto

Audemas jura nostra defendera—Latin for "We dare to defend our rights."

State Nickname

The "Yellowhammer State," because Alabama troops in the Confederate Army decorated their caps with yellowhammer feathers. Also called the "Cotton State" and "The Heart of Dixie."

Places

Alabama International Motor Speedway, Talladega

Alabama Space and Rocket Center, Huntsville

Ave Maria Grotto, Cullman

Azalea Trail, Mobile

Bellingrath Gardens, Mobile

Birmingham Zoo, Birmingham

Boll Weevil Monument, Enterprise

Cathedral Caverns, Grant

Chantilly Plantation House, Montgomery

De Soto Caverns, Childersburg

Dexter Avenue King Memorial Baptist Church, Montgomery

First "White House" of the Confederacy, Montgomery

Fort Conde/ Charlotte House, Mobile

Fort Morgan, Mobile Bay

George Washington Carver Museum, Tuskegee

Horseshoe Bend National Military Park, Dadeville

Indian Mound Museum, Florence

Ivy Green (Helen Keller's home), Tuscumbia

Jasmine Hill Garden, Mobile

Magnolia Springs, Baldwin County

Mobile Art Gallery, Mobile

Mound State Monument, Moundville

to See

Museum of Art,
Birmingham

Museum of Fine
Arts, Montgomery

Museum of the City
of Mobile, Mobile

Natural Bridge,
Haleyville

Oakleigh
Restoration and
Museum, Mobile

Oak Mountain State
Park, Birmingham

Old North Hull
Historical District,
Montgomery

Pioneer House
Museum, Moulton

Pope's Tavern,
Florence

Regar Museum of
Natural History,
Anniston

Russell Cave
National
Monument,
Bridgeport

Sequoyah Caverns,
Valley Head

Sloss Furnaces,
Birmingham

State Capitol,
Montgomery

Sturdivant
Museum, Selma

Tannehill State
Historical Park,
Bessemer

Tuskegee Institute
National Historical
Site, Tuskegee

U.S. Army
Aviation Museum,
Fort Rucker

USS Alabama/
Battleship Park,
Mobile Bay

Vestavia Temple
and Gardens,
Birmingham

W. C. Handy
Birthplace
and Museum,
Florence

State Flower

The camellia, Alabama's state flower, is a flowering evergreen shrub that produces five-inch-wide flowers of white, pink, and red. Camellias thrive in Alabama's warm climate.

State Bird

The yellowhammer is Alabama's state bird. Also known as the yellow-shafted flicker, this member of the finch family is about twelve inches long. It has yellow feathers beneath its wings and a bright red patch on its head.

State Tree

The Southern pine, which is actually the name for a family of coniferous (cone-bearing) evergreen trees that includes the loblolly, longleaf, and shortleaf pines.

Alabama History

American

c. 1400 Decline of mound-building Indian culture in Southeast

1519 Alonso Álvarez de Piñeda of Spain is first European to enter Mobile Bay

1540 Hernando de Soto travels through present-day Alabama

1559 Tristan de Luna leads colonizing attempt near Mobile

1702 First French settlement, Fort Louis, is built on the Mobile River

1711 Fort Louis moves to site near Mobile

1763 Control of Alabama region passes to Great Britain

1783 Most of present-day Alabama

comes under U.S. rule; Spain regains control of Mobile

1813 U.S. forces capture Mobile
• Creeks attack Fort Mims, sparking war with the U.S.

1814 Creek Nation gives up lands in Alabama after defeat in the Battle of Horseshoe Bend

1817 Congress organizes Alabama Territory

1819 Alabama becomes 22nd state

1838 Alabama's remaining Indians forced to leave state

1846 Alabama's capital moves to Montgomery

1861 Alabama secedes from Union and joins Confederate States of America;

1492 Christopher Columbus reaches the New World

1607 Jamestown (Virginia) founded by English colonists

1620 *Mayflower* arrives at Plymouth (Massachusetts)

1754–63 French and Indian War

1765 Parliament passes Stamp Act

1775–83 Revolutionary War

1776 Signing of the Declaration of Independence

1788–90 First congressional elections

1791 Bill of Rights added to U.S. Constitution

1803 Louisiana Purchase

1812–14 War of 1812

1820 Missouri Compromise

1836 Battle of the Alamo, Texas

1846–48 Mexican-American War

1849 California Gold Rush

1860 South Carolina secedes from Union

1861–65 Civil War

1862 Lincoln signs Homestead Act

1863 Emancipation Proclamation

1865 President Lincoln assassinated (April 14)

1865–77 Reconstruction in the South

1866 Civil Rights bill passed

1881 President James Garfield shot (July 2)

History

1896 First Ford automobile is made

1898–99 Spanish-American War

1901 President William McKinley is shot (Sept. 6)

1917 U.S. enters World War I

1922 Nineteenth Amendment passed, giving women the vote

1929 U.S. stock market crash; Great Depression begins

1933 Franklin D. Roosevelt becomes president; begins New Deal

1941 Japanese attack Pearl Harbor (Dec. 7); U.S. enters World War II

1945 U.S. drops atomic bomb on Hiroshima and Nagasaki; Japan surrenders, ending World War II

1963 President Kennedy assassinated (November 22)

1964 Civil Rights Act passed

1965–73 Vietnam War

1968 Martin Luther King, Jr., shot in Memphis (April 4)

1974 President Richard Nixon resigns because of Watergate scandal

1979–81 Hostage crisis in Iran: 52 Americans held captive for 444 days

1989 End of U.S.-Soviet cold war

1991 Gulf War

1993 U.S. signs North American Free Trade Agreement with Canada and Mexico

Alabama History

Montgomery is first Confederate capital

1864 Union fleet blocks Mobile Bay during Civil War

1868 Alabama is re-admitted to Union

1880 First blast furnace begins operation at Birmingham; start of state's iron and steel industry

1881 Booker T. Washington founds Tuskegee Institute

1901 New state constitution adopted

1933 Tennessee Valley Authority (TVA) established

1950 U.S. rocket and space program established at Redstone Arsenal in Huntsville

1955 Montgomery Bus Boycott begins

1956 Montgomery buses integrated

1960 The George C. Marshall Space Flight Center opens in Huntsville

1963 African-American students admitted to University of Alabama
•Four African-American children killed in racially motivated bombing in Birmingham

1965 Martin Luther King, Jr., leads civil rights march from Selma to Montgomery

1974 George Wallace elected governor for third term; he returns to office for a fourth term in 1982

1987 Guy Hunt becomes Alabama's first Republican governor since Reconstruction

Alexander McGillivray (c. 1759–93) The son of a Scottish trader and a Creek mother, McGillivray established ties with the British, French, and American governments in his effort to preserve Creek independence.

William Rufus Devane King (1786–1853) King helped draft Alabama's state constitution and served as U.S. senator from the state for many years. In 1853 he became vice president of the United States.

Daniel Pratt (1799–1873) Pratt did much to establish the Cotton Kingdom in Alabama. He began manufacturing cotton gins in 1834, and within a decade he was the leading maker of gins in the state. He also built one of the state's first cotton mills.

Daniel Pratt

Raphael Semmes (1809–77) The Confederacy's most successful naval officer, Semmes commanded the warship *Alabama*, which captured or sunk scores of Union merchant ships.

William Lowndes Yancey (1814–63) Yancey was a strong supporter of slavery and "Southern rights." After Alabama's secession, he served as a Confederate diplomat in Europe and as a senator in the Confederate Congress.

Julia Tutwiler (1841–1916) A champion of educational opportunities for women, Tutwiler founded several schools in Alabama and fought to have women admitted to the state university. She also wrote the words to "Alabama," the state song.

Booker T. Washington (1856–1915) A writer, educator, and speaker, Washington was one of the most influential African-American leaders of the late 19th and early 20th centuries. In 1881 he founded the Tuskegee Institute.

George Washington Carver (c. 1861–1943) A brilliant

scientist and educator, Carver became Tuskegee Institute's director of agricultural research in 1896. He developed hundreds of uses for such common crops as peanuts and sweet potatoes, greatly expanding the productivity of Southern agriculture.

William Christopher (W.C.) Handy (1873–1958) Often called "the father of the blues," this pioneering musician and composer was born in Florence. Handy's compositions had a great influence on the development of jazz as an American art form.

Helen Keller (1880–1968) Although left blind and deaf in childhood, Tuscumbia-born Keller became a well-known writer, educator, and supporter of many social causes.

Hugo Lafayette Black (1886–1971) Black served as U.S. senator from Alabama (1927–37) before his appointment to the Supreme Court. He was a major supporter of civil rights in his forty-four years on the court.

Wernher von Braun (1912–77) The leading German rocket engineer of World

War II, von Braun was captured by U.S. forces in 1945. In 1950, he moved to Alabama to work on American rocket projects, including the *Apollo 11* moon landing in 1969.

Jesse Owens (1913–80) One of the 20th century's greatest track-and-field athletes and a Danville native, Owens won four gold medals at the 1936 Berlin Olympics.

Paul "Bear" Bryant (1913–83) One of college football's greatest coaches, Bryant led the University of Alabama's "Crimson Tide" to 323 victories.

Rosa Parks (b. 1913) Parks's refusal to move to the back of a Montgomery bus sparked the Montgomery Bus Boycott. She remained active in the civil rights movement and in 1979 was awarded the NAACP's Spingarn Medal.

Nathaniel "Nat King" Cole (1919–65) Known for his sentimental yet sophisticated ballads, this Montgomery-born singer and musician was the first African-American entertainer to have his own national radio and television shows.

George Corley Wallace (b. 1919) A four-term governor of Alabama, Wallace opposed the desegregation movement in the early 1960s. He ran for president in 1968 and was crippled in an assassination attempt while again campaigning for the presidency in 1972. In his later years, Wallace claimed to have changed his attitudes about race, and he won the support of many African-American Alabamians.

Hank Williams (1923–53) Born in Georgiana, Williams became country music's greatest star after joining the Grand Ole Opry in 1949. His son, Hank Williams, Jr., (b. 1949) is also a famous country musician.

Nelle (Harper) Lee (b. 1926) One of Alabama's best-known writers, Lee won the 1960 Pulitzer Prize for fiction for her novel *To Kill a Mockingbird*, an examination of racial attitudes in a small Alabama town.

Martin Luther King, Jr. (1929–68) Born in Georgia, this great civil rights leader first gained national attention as the organizer of the successful Montgomery Bus Boycott (1955–56); he returned to Alabama to lead the 1965

Jesse Owens

protest march from Selma to Montgomery. Awarded the Nobel Peace Prize in 1964, King was assassinated in Memphis, Tennessee, in 1968.

Henry Louis "Hank" Aaron (b. 1934) On April 8, 1974, this Mobile-born baseball player hit his 714th home run, breaking the long-standing record set by Babe Ruth. Aaron ended his major-league career with 755 runs.

Bo Jackson (b. 1963) Jackson won the 1985 Heisman Trophy as a player on Auburn University's football team. He became one of the best pro athletes of the 1980s, playing on both the Los Angeles Raiders football team and the Kansas City Royals baseball team.

Pictures in this volume:

Alabama Bureau of Tourism & Travel: 2
(Dan Brothers)

Copyright *The Birmingham News*. All rights
reserved. Reprinted by permission: 44

Dover: 9 (top), 25, 36 (bottom)

Library of Congress: 7, 10, 11, 12-13, 17, 18
(top), 18 (bottom), 19, 20, 21, 24, 26, 28, 29, 31,
32, 33, 34 (top), 34 (bottom), 35, 39, 41 (top),
43, 45, 47 (top), 60

Media Projects Archives: 36 (top), 38, 48, 49, 53

Mobile Chamber of Commerce: 51

Mobile Public Library Collection: 15

Mound State Monument: 9 (bottom)

National Archives: 41 (bottom), 61

National Aeronautics and Space Administration: 42

Peter Pettus: 47 (bottom)

U.S. Space and Rocket Center: 52 (Bob Gathany)

The Woolaroc Museum, Bartlesville, Oklahoma:
22-23

About the author:

Charles A. Wills is a writer, editor, and consultant
specializing in American history. He has written,
edited, or contributed to more than thirty books,
including many volumes in The Millbrook Press's
*American Albums from the Collections of the
Library of Congress* series. Wills lives in Dutchess
County, New York.

Suggested reading:

Benjamin, Anne, *Young Rosa Parks: A Civil Rights
Heroine*, Mahwah, NJ: Troll Associates, 1995

Carpenter, Allan, *The New Enchantment of
America: Alabama*, Chicago: Childrens Press,
1978

Hamilton, Virginia Van der Veer, *Alabama: A
History*, New York: Norton, 1984

King, Martin Luther, Jr., *Letter from the
Birmingham Jail*, San Francisco: HarperCollins
San Francisco, 1994

Lesher, Stephan, *George Wallace: American
Populist*, Reading, MA: Addison-Wesley, 1994

McNair, Sylvia, *America the Beautiful: Alabama*,
Chicago: Childrens Press, 1989

Norrell, Robert, *The Alabama Story*, Tuscaloosa,
AL: The Yellowhammer Press, 1993

Norrell, Robert, *The Making of Modern Alabama*,
Tuscaloosa, AL: The Yellowhammer Press, 1993

Thompson, Kathleen, *Portrait of America:
Alabama*, Milwaukee, WI: Raintree Publishers,
1988

For more information contact:

Alabama Bureau of Travel & Tourism
401 Adams Avenue
Montgomery, AL 36104-4331
Tel. (800) 252-2262

Alabama Department of Archives and History
624 Washington Avenue
Montgomery, Alabama 36130-3601
Tel. (205) 242-4435

INDEX